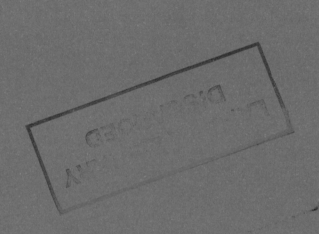

Facts About Countries
India

Lizann Flatt

FRANKLIN WATTS
LONDON•SYDNEY

C409287605

First published in 2005 by
Franklin Watts
96 Leonard Street, London
EC2A 4XD

Franklin Watts Australia
Level 17/207 Kent Street
Sydney NSW 2000

Facts About Countries is based on the Country
Files series published by Franklin Watts. It is
produced for Franklin Watts by Bender
Richardson White, PO Box 266, Uxbridge, UK.
Editors: Lionel Bender, Angela Royston
Designer and Page Make-up: Ben White
Picture Researcher: Cathy Stastny
Cover Make-up: Mike Pilley, Radius
Production: Kim Richardson

Graphics and Maps: Stefan Chabluk
Educational Advisor: Prue Goodwin, Institute of
Education, The University of Reading
Consultant: Dr Terry Jennings, a former
geography teacher and university lecturer. He is
now a full-time writer of children's geography
and science books.

A CIP catalogue record for this book is available
from the British Library.

ISBN 0-7496-6030-9
Dewey Classification 915.4

Printed in China

Picture Credits

Pages: 1: PhotoDisc Inc./Glen Allison. 3: PhotoDisc
Inc./Santokh Kochar. 4: Hutchison Photo
Library/David Culverd. 7: PhotoDisc Inc./Santokh
Kochar. 8: Hutchison Photo Library/Jeremy Horner.
9: Hutchison Photo Library/Juliet Highet.10: PhotoDisc
Inc./Santokh Kochar. 10-11: Hutchison Photo Library.
12 top: Hutchison Photo Library/Jeremy Horner.
12-13 bottom: Hutchison Photo Library/Nigara Film
Workshop. 15 and 16: Hutchison Photo Library/Jeremy
Horner. 18: Hutchison Photo Library/Liba Taylor.
19: Hutchison Photo Library/Nancy Durrell McKenna.
20: Eye Ubiquitous/David Cumming. 21: Yann Arthus-
Bertrand/CORBIS Pictures. 22 top: Hutchison Photo
Library/M. Jelliffe. 22 bottom: Hutchison Photo Library.
24: Hutchison Photo Library/Maurice Harvey.
25: Hutchison Photo Library. 26 top: Hutchison Photo
Library/Jeremy Horner. 26 bottom: James Davis Travel
Photography/James Davis. 28-29: PhotoDisc Inc./Ingo
Jezierski. 30: PhotoDisc Inc./Santokh Kochar.
31: PhotoDisc Inc./Ingo Jezierski.
Cover photo: Eye Ubiquitous Photo Library.

The Author

Lizann Flatt is an award-winning author and editor of children's non-fiction books and magazines.

Note to parents and teachers

Every effort has been made by the Publishers to ensure
that the websites in this book are suitable for children,
that they are of the highest educational value, and that
they contain no inappropriate or offensive material.
However, because of the nature of the Internet, it is
impossible to guarantee that the contents of these sites
will not be altered. We strongly advise that Internet
access is supervised by a responsible adult.

Contents

Welcome to India

The Republic of India is the largest country in South Asia. Its people call it Bharat. India has the second largest population in the world.

A rich and varied land

India has a long history. There are many temples and holy sites in India. The country is known for its textiles, tea and diamonds. India has large cities and many small villages. Poor people live next to rich people.

Below. **Dal Lake in Kashmir in northern India. The boats are lined up waiting for tourists to hire them.**

4

AFGHANISTAN

CHINA

PAKISTAN

Indus

Leh

Amritsar

35°N
70°E 75°E 80°E 85°E 90°E 95°E
30°N
25°N
20°N
15°N
10°N

GREAT INDIAN DESERT

New Delhi

Jaipur

Agra

Yamuna

Lucknow

INDO-GANGETIC PLAIN

Varanasi

Ganga (Ganges)

H I M A L A Y A S

NEPAL

BHUTAN

Brahmaputra

BANGLADESH

Tropic of Cancer

MYANMAR

Ahmedabad

VINDHYA MOUNTAINS

Narmada

Surat

I N D I A

Nagpur

DECCAN PLATEAU

Godavari

Calcutta

Mumbai

Hyderabad

Krishna

EASTERN GHATS

WESTERN GHATS

Goa

Penner

BAY OF BENGAL

ARABIAN SEA

N
W E
S

Bangalore

Mysore

Chennai

Pondicherry

Lakshadweep (Laccadive) Islands

Madurai

Thiruvananthapuram

SRI LANKA

INDIAN OCEAN

Andaman Islands

Nicobar Islands

Legend:
- Desert
- Mountains
- Grassland and farming
- □ Capital ○ Major city
- —— Country boundary
- - - - Disputed boundary

0   500 Miles
0   750 Kilometres

5

The Land

Animals and Plants

India has a many different places where animals and plants live, including mountains, rivers, forests, plains and deserts. This means it has a wide variety of Asian animals and plants.

Mammals:
Asiatic lion, leopard, tiger, Indian elephant, rhinoceros, antelope, wild buffalo, yak, Indian bison, hyena, jackal, monkey, bear and Gangetic dolphin.

Birds:
myna bird, peacock, vulture, crow, pigeon, crane and stork.

Reptiles:
python, cobra, gecko and crocodile.

Plants:
palm tree, bamboo, maple, rhododendron, ebony, teak, banyan, fruit trees such as mango, jackfruit, papaya and banana.

India is made up of three areas: The Himalaya mountains, the Indo-Gangetic Plain and the Peninsula.

The Himalayas
The Himalaya mountains are covered with snow, but tropical plants, rice and fruit trees grow in the valleys.

The Indo-Gangetic Plain
This area is mainly farmland and it is where most people live. Three great rivers flow across the plain – the Indus, Ganga and Brahmaputra rivers.

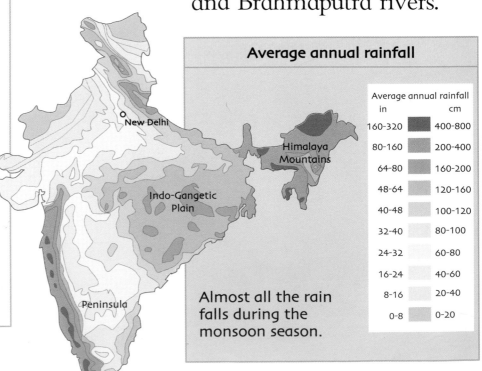

Average annual rainfall

Average annual rainfall	
in	cm
160-320	400-800
80-160	200-400
64-80	160-200
48-64	120-160
40-48	100-120
32-40	80-100
24-32	60-80
16-24	40-60
8-16	20-40
0-8	0-20

New Delhi

Himalaya Mountains

Indo-Gangetic Plain

Peninsula

Almost all the rain falls during the monsoon season.

6

Above. The city of Pushkar in Rajasthan, north-west India. The city is on the edge of the Great Indian Desert. This desert is the driest part of India and is on the Indo-Gangetic Plain.

Below. Highest and lowest temperatures for Calcutta and Amritsar.

The Peninsula

The Peninsula stretches to the southern tip of India. The Western Ghats and the Eastern Ghats run on each side of the coast. There are many forests on the Peninsula.

Climate

India has three seasons: winter (November to March), summer (April to June) and the monsoon (July to October). During the monsoon it rains every day in most places.

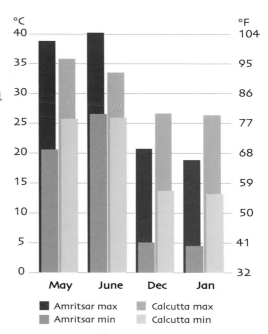

■ Amritsar max   ■ Calcutta max
■ Amritsar min   ■ Calcutta min

7

The People

Just over 1 billion people live in India – only China has more people. India's culture is more than 4,500 years old.

Multicultural

Over its long history, many different peoples have settled in or invaded India. Most of them came overland from the north-east and north-west. Each of them added to the culture and languages of India. They helped to make the mixed and different peoples of India today.

Many languages

Hindi is the national language of India, but there are 18 official languages. Most people know at least one official language. English is the main language used by businesses and the government.

Female   Male

48%   52%

Above. **India has more men than women.**

Below. **Women wash themselves and their clothes in a river. India's great rivers play an important part in religion and in everyday life.**

8

 ## Ancient History

Two of Asia's oldest cultures come from India. The Indus Valley civilization was successful in the north for nearly 1,000 years. When the Aryans invaded in around 1500 BCE, it is thought that people from the Indus Valley were pushed out. They formed the Dravidian civilization in central and southern India.

Left. **People at a street market in Orissa state, east India. The market is outside a Hindu temple.**

 ## Web Search ▶▶

▶ **www.censusindia.net/**
Facts and figures about the population.

▶ **http://indiaimage.nic.in/**
India's National Information Centre, with links to many government websites.

▶ **www.mapsofindia.com/**
Maps of India.

▶ **www.indianmuseum-calcutta. org/**
Museum showing Indian traditions, customs and handicrafts.

Town and Country Life

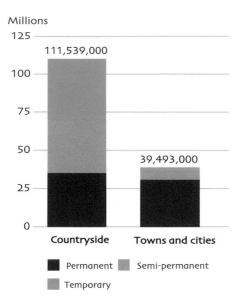

Millions

Above. **The number of different kinds of homes in cities and villages.**

Most Indians live in villages and small towns in the countryside. However, many young people are moving to the cities to find work and a better life.

City houses with servants

Cities are overcrowded but the houses have piped water and electricity. Rich families have large houses and several servants. Middle-class families live in apartments or small houses.

Below. **In the countryside, most people work on the land. They often use animals instead of machines.**

Villages

In the villages, rich families may have two-storey brick houses with electricity and piped water. Poor families have houses made from mud and straw or wood and palm leaves. Not all villages have electricity, and many houses have no piped water. Instead, people pump drinking water from wells and carry it to their homes. They bathe and wash their clothes in nearby lakes or streams.

Above. **City homes with piped drinking water.**

Above. **Village homes with piped drinking water.**

Below. **In big cities such as Mumbai, many poor people live in slums. They make shelters using cardboard and sheets of iron.**

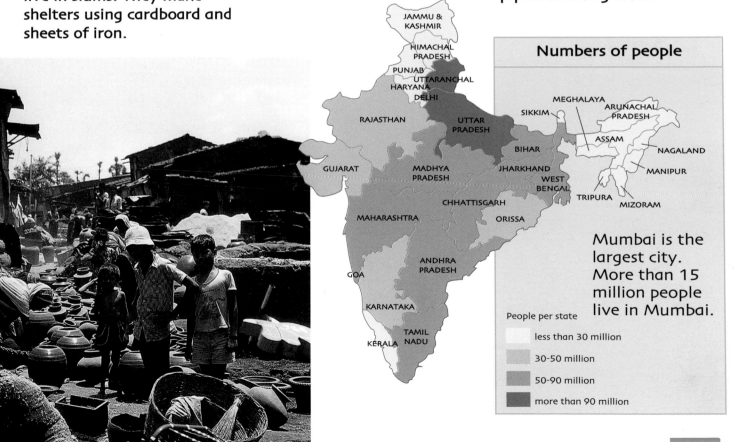

Numbers of people

JAMMU & KASHMIR

HIMACHAL PRADESH

PUNJAB

UTTARANCHAL

HARYANA

DELHI

RAJASTHAN

UTTAR PRADESH

MEGHALAYA

SIKKIM

ARUNACHAL PRADESH

ASSAM

BIHAR

NAGALAND

GUJARAT

MADHYA PRADESH

JHARKHAND

MANIPUR

WEST BENGAL

TRIPURA

CHHATTISGARH

MIZORAM

MAHARASHTRA

ORISSA

ANDHRA PRADESH

GOA

KARNATAKA

TAMIL NADU

KERALA

Mumbai is the largest city. More than 15 million people live in Mumbai.

People per state

less than 30 million

30-50 million

50-90 million

more than 90 million

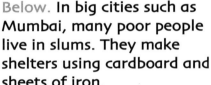

11

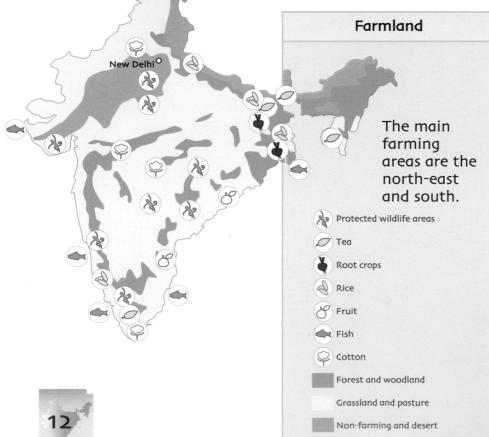

New Delhi

Farmland

The main farming areas are the north-east and south.

- Protected wildlife areas
- Tea
- Root crops
- Rice
- Fruit
- Fish
- Cotton
- Forest and woodland
- Grassland and pasture
- Non-farming and desert

Above. **Tea leaves are picked by hand on tea plantations in Darjeeling, northern India.**

Farming and Fishing

More than half the people in India work in farming. India produces a lot of milk, sugar, fruit and grain. Fishing is important along the coast.

Farming and food

Farmers grow rice and wheat all year round. They also grow vegetables, spices and fruits. Factories produce biscuits, chocolate, pasta and fizzy drinks.

Fishing

India's fishermen catch the sixth largest amount of fish in the world. Most of the fish are frozen or tinned and then sold to other countries. Some fish are made into food for chickens.

DATABASE

Production each year

Milk   74,700,000 tonnes
Fish   5,260,000 tonnes
Meat   4,500,000 tonnes
Sugar-cane 295,700,000 tonnes
Bread   1,500,000 tonnes
Biscuits 1,100,000 tonnes
Cocoa products such as chocolate 34,000 tonnes

Eggs   30,150,000,000

Cotton   12,200,000 bales
Jute & hemp   9,700,000 bales
Fizzy drinks   6,320,000,000 bottles

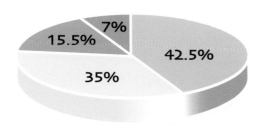

- Wheat 70.78 million tonnes
- Other cereals 31.4 million tonnes
- Peas, beans, pulses 14.8 million tonnes
- Rice 86 million tonnes

Above. **Amount of each crop produced in India.**

Left. **Local fishermen bring in their catch on a beach in the state of Kerala.**

13

Resources and Industry

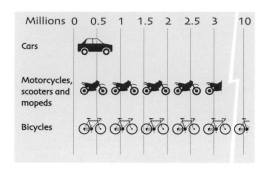

Above. **Number of road vehicles made each year.**

India is rich in many minerals. It uses these and other resources to make things. India is one of the largest industrial countries in the world.

Resources

India's largest resource is coal. It has enough coal to last 100 years. India is also the world's largest producer of mica, which is used in industry. Other major resources include iron ore, bauxite, lignite, crude oil, natural gas and diamonds.

Energy

India produces lots of energy. All cities and most villages are now supplied with electricity. Most power is made from coal, but India also has hydroelectric and nuclear power plants. However, the amount of electricity needed is greater than the amount made, so power blackouts are common. Some villagers still have to collect wood from forests, and use waste and cow dung to burn as fuels.

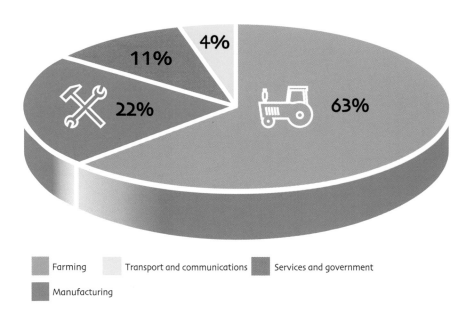

Farming   Transport and communications   Services and government

Manufacturing

Above. **Percentages of workers in major industries.**

14

Industries

About 20 million people work in India's textile industry. They make thread, cloth, clothes and carpets. Other important industries include leather, steel, cars, food, electronics and computer software.

Above. **Trees in Tamil Nadu in southern India are cut down and used for timber.**

Below. **Weight of industrial products made each year.**

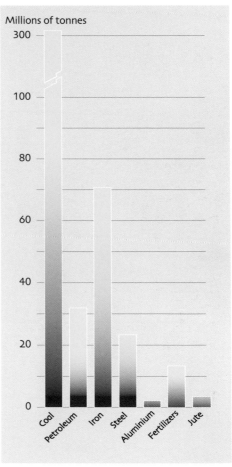

Resources and Industry

Most mines and factories are in the north-east, central and coastal areas of India.

- Steel
- Railroad equipment
- Oil
- Mining
- Coal

New Delhi O

Transport

Most people use buses and trains to travel across India. A growing number of people travel by car. Air travel is also becoming more popular.

Roads

India has more than 3 million kilometres of roads, but many roads are narrow and crowded. The government is planning to build new main roads and motorways.

 Railway Network

India has the second largest rail network in the world. Every day, trains carry 12 million people and more than a million tonnes of freight. High-speed trains connect New Delhi with other major cities.

Below. **Railway workers repair tracks at Jaisalmer in Rajasthan.**

16

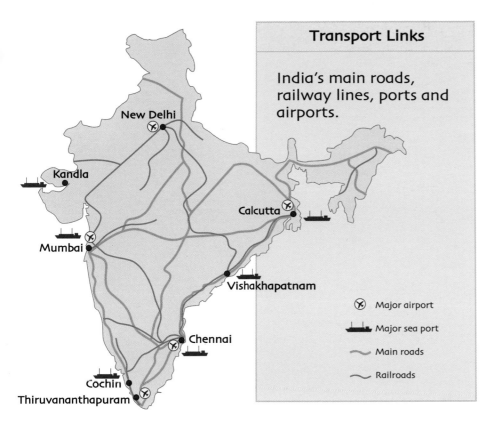

Transport Links

India's main roads, railway lines, ports and airports.

New Delhi
Kandla
Calcutta
Mumbai
Vishakhapatnam
Chennai
Cochin
Thiruvananthapuram

- ⊗ Major airport
- ⛴ Major sea port
- 〰 Main roads
- 〰 Railroads

City Transport

All of the major cities and towns have buses, trains, trams, taxis and auto-rickshaws for people to use. Calcutta and New Delhi have underground railways, too.

Below. Motor vehicles bought in India.

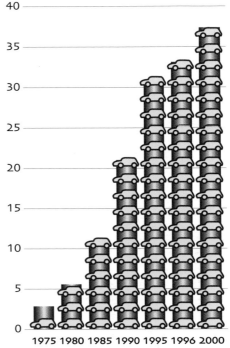

Millions

1975 1980 1985 1990 1995 1996 2000

Ships

India has many huge oil tankers and cargo ships. Hundreds of smaller ships work along the coast. In the states of Kerala and West Bengal, barges, ships and ferries carry people and goods up and down the rivers.

Air travel

India has about 350 airports. Several aeroplanes fly each day between the major cities. New Delhi and Mumbai are the main international airports, with flights to other Asian countries and Europe.

Web Search ▶▶

▶ www.mapsofindia.com/distances
Distances and routes between most cities and major towns.

▶ www.indianrail.gov.in
India's railway system.

▶ www.airindia.com
India's major airlines.

17

Education

Education in India is getting better. In 1951 only 18 per cent of the people could read. By 2000, 58 per cent could read.

Schools

The government provides free schooling for all children between the ages of 6 and 14. Even so, some families are so poor the children have to work instead of going to school. The school day lasts from 9.00 a.m. to 3.30 p.m. After the age of 14, many children go to secondary school. Children study languages, maths, science, geography, history and physical education.

Below. **Pupils at primary school (aged 6 to 10 years).**

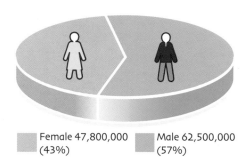

Female 47,800,000 (43%) Male 62,500,000 (57%)

Below. **Pupils at middle school (aged 11 to 14 years).**

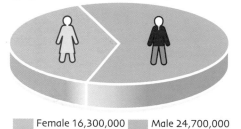

Female 16,300,000 (39.7%) Male 24,700,000 (60.3%)

Below. **Pupils at secondary school (aged 14+ years).**

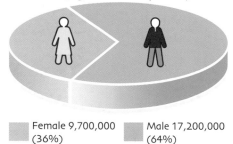

Female 9,700,000 (36%) Male 17,200,000 (64%)

Below. **Women learning to read and write at a class for adults. The government is helping many adults to learn new skills so everyone is better educated.**

18

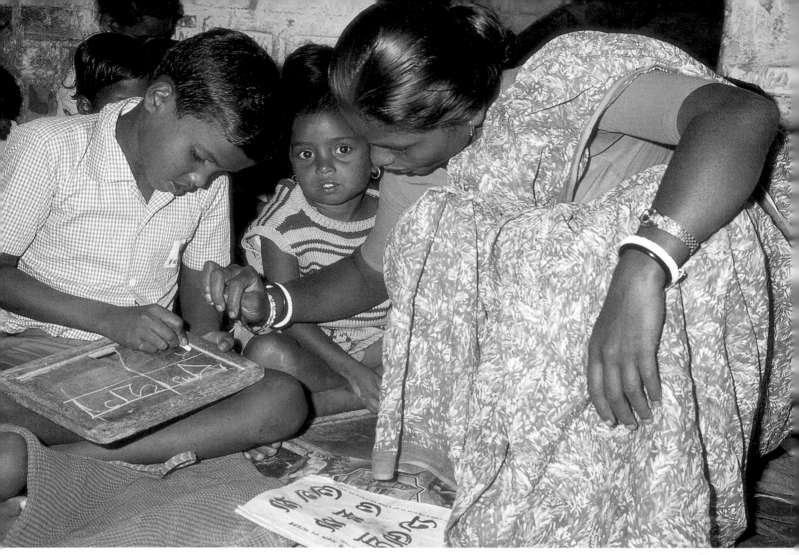

Children in cities often go to private schools, which their parents must pay for. After secondary school, children can go university. Many students study at universities abroad.

Above. Many village schools use slate boards and chalk for writing instead of paper and pens.

Left. The number of men and women who go to university in India.

Web Search ►►

► www.goidirectory.nic.in/
Government information on education.

0   1.0   2.0   3.0   4.0 Millions

19

Sport and Leisure

Indians play many different sports. Hockey and cricket are the most popular.

Hockey

Hockey is India's national sport. The national hockey team has won eight gold medals at the Olympic Games.

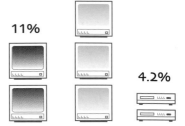

28%

11%

4.2%

Below. Several games of cricket are being played in this park in Calcutta.

Above. Households with colour TVs, black and white TVs and video players.

Other sports

Children play cricket in parks and on the streets. Everyone follows important matches on TV or radio. Other sports include tennis, chess, archery and judo. Elephant racing and camel racing are also popular.

Leisure activities

Rich people in India like to go to the theatre and cinema. Poorer people who do not have money to do this watch television instead. Often, people who do not own a TV go to the house of someone who does.

Left. Polo is played on horseback with a ball and long sticks. The game is also played in Britain and other countries.

Above. A Hindu holy man
and a tourist ride on an
elephant through the streets
of Udaipur, Rajasthan.

Right. Hindu holy men
meditate beside the River
Ganga at Varanasi.

Daily Life and Religion

Most Indian people's life is centered around religion. The main religions in India are Hinduism, Islam, Buddhism and Sikhism.

Religion

There are temples, holy sites and religious statues all over India. Hindus worship in their homes as well as in temples. Many homes have a shrine to one of the Hindu gods. Muslims are followers of Islam. They pray five times each day and may go to their mosque on Fridays. The most holy Sikh temple is in Amritsar in the north-west. Buddhists worship in temples and make offerings at shrines and monasteries.

Shopping

Bazaars, or local markets, are everywhere. The stalls sell almost everything, from food and clothes to sweets and toys. In private shops, people bargain for the price of what they buy. But government shops in the cities sell goods at fixed prices. The largest cities also have shopping malls.

Below. How families spend their money each year.

%
0 5 10 15 20 25 30 35 40 45 50

Food, beverages and tobacco
Clothing and shoes
Rent, fuel and electricity
Furniture, appliances and services
Medical care
Transport and communication
Leisure, education and cultural services
Other goods and services

Web Search ▶▶

▶ http://indiaimage.nic.in/
India's National Information Centre.

▶ www.indiaserver.com/
Official news stories.

23

Arts and Media

DATABASE

Top Tourist Destinations
1. The Taj Mahal, Agra
2. New Delhi, the capital city
3. Jaipur in Rajasthan
4. Goa's golden beaches and old city
5. Leh and other towns in the Himalayas
6. Varanasi – Hindu pilgrimage site
7. Kerala – beaches and beautiful villages
8. Chennai and other temple cities
9. Mumbai (Bombay)
10. Wildlife parks

Indian cinema is world-famous. Music, theatre, television, radio and other forms of art are also important.

Radio, television and newspapers

All India Radio (AIR) has 198 radio stations, and 90 per cent of people watch national television. Many Indians also watch satellite and cable TV. Most newspapers are published in Hindi.

Below. **A concert hall in Chennai, a temple city in Tamil Nadu.**

24

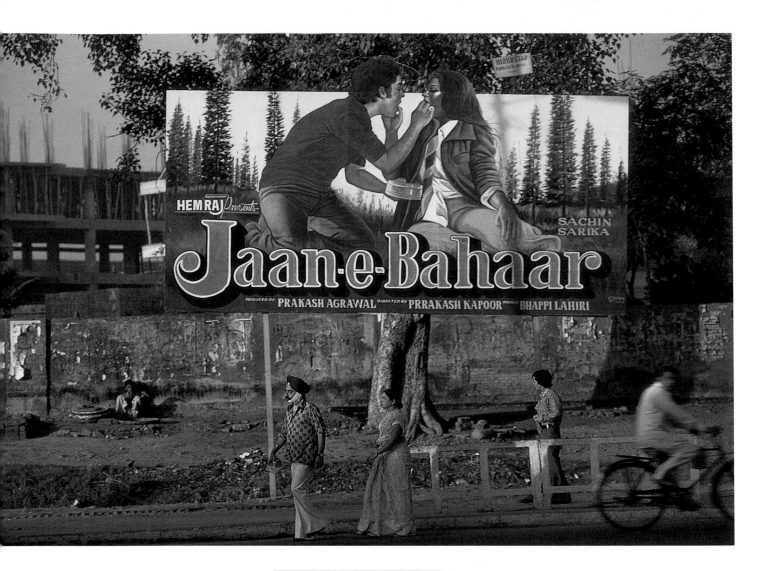

Tourists

India has become a popular place to visit. More than 2 million tourists travel to India each year. They go to see ancient temples, colourful fairs and golden beaches.

Bollywood

More films are made in India (over 900 every year) than in Hollywood, USA. Watching movies is very popular and there are cinemas everywhere.

The city of Mumbai is nicknamed 'Bollywood' because it is the centre of the Indian film industry.

Above. An advertisement for a 'Bollywood' film.

Web Search ▶▶

▶ www.webindia.com/
Indian music, crafts and dance.

▶ www.ddindia.com/
Doordarshan Indian TV station.

▶ www.timesofindia.com/
Times of India newspaper.

▶ www.hinduonline.com/
The Hindu newspaper site.

25

Government

The modern Republic of India was founded in 1947. The leaders of the country are the president, the vice president and the prime minister.

The president

The president is the head of state and commander-in-chief of the armed forces. He or she works with a council of ministers and advisors.

Above. India Gate is a World War I memorial. It is in New Delhi, the capital city of India.

Below. Government House in Bangalore, the capital city of the state of Karnataka.

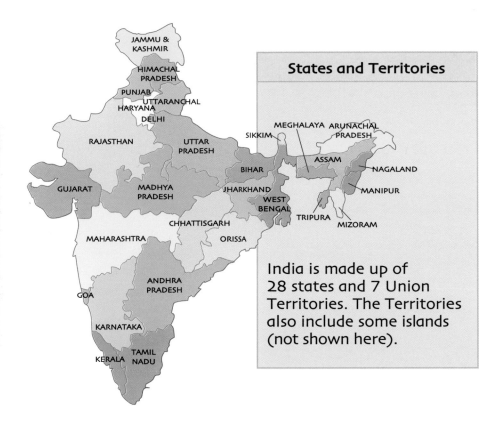

States and Territories

India is made up of 28 states and 7 Union Territories. The Territories also include some islands (not shown here).

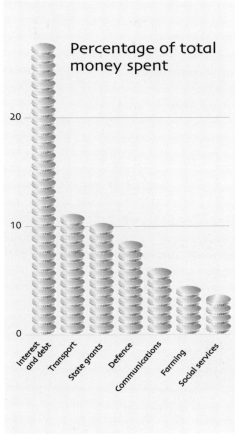

Below. **How the Indian government spends money each year.**

Percentage of total money spent

Elections

All Indian citizens can vote from the age of 18. They elect members to represent them in the Lok Sabha (House of the People). The prime minister is the leader of the political party that wins the most votes in a national election. The prime minister and the council of ministers run the country.

State government

Each state has its own governors who are elected by the ordinary people. These governors elect people to sit in the national Council of States.

Web Search ▶▶

▶ www.indiabudget.nic.in/
How the government spends its money

▶ www.goidirectory.nic.in/
Directory of government websites.

▶ www.pib.nic.in/
India's Press Information Bureau.

Place in the World

Historical Events – up to 1600

8500 BCE–2500 BCE Farming settlements in the general area of the Indus Valley

2000 BCE Indus Valley civilization disappears

1500 BCE Aryan settlers move in

1200–500 BCE Early Hindu religious texts written

570–450 BCE Spread of Buddhism and Jainism

320 –232 BCE Mauryan Dynasty dominates most of India

CE 319–467 Gupta Empire

600–1192 Regional kingdoms at strongest

1206 Islamic dynasty; various Sultans rule

1469-1538 Rise of Sikhism

1526-1707 Mogul Empire

1542 First Christian missionary arrives

India's civilizations are thousands of years old, but the modern Republic of India is still quite young.

Making progress

The Indian government is trying to make the electricity and transport systems better. It also wants more people to be educated.

International links

India is part of such international organizations as the United Nations, the World Health Organization and Interpol, an international police group. India is also a member of organizations that encourage countries in Asia to work together. These organizations try to help the poor and stop fighting at the borders. India has recently increased its trade with the rest of the world. This has made the country richer.

Historical Events – from 1600

1757 British East India Company gains control of parts of India

1857 British government takes control of India from East India Company

1906 Muslim League established in India

1920 Mahatma Gandhi begins non-violent campaign against British rule

1947 Muslim League demands a separate Muslim country. 15 August, independence from Great Britain; Pakistan, a Muslim country, is created

1948 Mahatma Gandhi is killed

1950 January 26, India becomes a republic

2004 Huge tidal wave hits south-east coast, killing many thousands

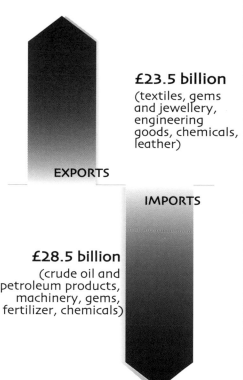

£23.5 billion
(textiles, gems and jewellery, engineering goods, chemicals, leather)

EXPORTS

IMPORTS

£28.5 billion
(crude oil and petroleum products, machinery, gems, fertilizer, chemicals)

Above. India's imports and exports.

Left. The Taj Mahal in Agra. It is the tomb of an Indian empress who died in 1631.

29

Area:
3,287,263 sq km

Population size:
846,300,000 (1991 Census); 1,000,100,000 (2000 estimate)

Capital city:
New Delhi

Other major cities:
Mumbai, Calcutta, Chennai, Bangalore, Hyderabad

Longest Rivers:
Brahmaputra (2,900km), Indus (2,900km), Ganga (2,510km)

Highest mountain:
Kanchenjunga (8,598m)

Currency:
Indian rupees (Rs)
1 rupee = 100 paise
£1 = Rs 61.5 approximately

Flag:
An orange, white and green horizontal bands. The white band has a blue wheel (or chakra) centred in it.

Languages:
18 official languages including Hindi, Bengali, Urdu, Gujarati, Punjabi. English commonly used and understood.

Major resources:
coal, mica, iron ore, bauxite, lignite, aluminium, chromite, manganese, titanium, crude oil, natural gas, diamonds and limestone.

Major exports:
textiles, gems and jewellery, machinery, chemicals, leather, marine products, rice, tea.

National holidays and major events:
January 26: Republic Day
May 1: May Day/Labour Day
August 15: Independence Day
October 2: Mahatma Gandhi's Birthday
December 25: Christmas Day

Religions:
Religions practised include Hinduism, Islam, Buddhism, Jainism, Sikhism, Christianity, Zoroastrianism, Judaism

Key Words

AUTO-RICKSHAWS
Small passenger vehicles powered by motor scooters.

CIVILIZATION
A group of people with its own culture, art, way of life and government.

CLIMATE
The type of weather a place usually has at different times of the year.

CULTURE
A group of people practising the same traditions for many generations.

EMPIRE
A group of countries or lands ruled by a single country.

EXPORTS
Goods sold to a foreign country.

GOVERNMENT
The group of people that runs a country, making new laws, raising taxes and organizing health, education, transport and other national systems.

HYDROELECTRIC POWER
Electrical power generated from flowing water.

IMPORTS
Goods bought from a foreign country.

INDUSTRY
Mines, factories and businesses that make money.

JUTE
A plant used to make mats, sacks and string.

MINERAL
The form in which metals and other resources occur in rocks and in the soil.

MONSOON
Wind that blows from the sea and brings heavy rainy.

REPUBLIC
A country whose head of state is elected to govern.

PLANTATIONS
Areas of farmland where trees and shrubs are grown for their fruit and leaves.

RESOURCES
A country's supplies of energy, natural materials and minerals.

SLUMS
Areas of dirty, overcrowded houses and unpaved streets.

STATE
Part of a country that has its own government but is part of the national government.

TERRITORIES
Areas of land governed by a country.

TROPICAL
The part of the Earth that lies between the Tropic of Cancer and the Tropic of Capricorn: 'tropical' can also mean the hot and damp weather of that region.

31

Index